The Mechanics of English

S0-AYH-784

Introduction

When God created you, He gave you the ability to learn how to *read*, to *write*, to *speak*, and to *listen*. The language arts LIFEPACs you have used this year have helped you to develop these language skills. In this LIFEPAC® you will concentrate on your writing ability.

To improve your skills in the art of writing, you need to understand certain basic rules that will simplify the writing process. The memorization of rules, however, is meaningless without applying those rules in your day-to-day use of written language. Everyone wishes to be understood; and, to properly communicate ideas to others, one must draw from a reserve of grammatical and mechanical skills. By the time you have completed this LIFEPAC, you should feel more confident in your ability to express yourself clearly and precisely in writing.

You will first study the correct use of capitalization. Then you will study when and how to use internal punctuation such as the apostrophe, quotation marks, parentheses, hyphen, and the comma. You will also study about modifiers and how to use them when you write.

The use of coordination and subordination is not for beginners. At your level of study, you are ready to learn how to use these writing concepts. You will study them in the last section of this LIFEPAC. Do your best to master all areas of study because they are skills you will use for the rest of your life.

Objectives

Read these objectives. The objectives tell you what you will be able to do when you have successfully completed this LIFEPAC. When you have finished this LIFEPAC, you should be able to:

1. Capitalize words correctly.

2. Identify and correctly use the following internal punctuation: apostrophe, quotation marks, parentheses, and hyphen.

3. Explain the correct use of commas in introductory words and phrases, with coordinating conjunctions, with nonessential elements, and in series.

4. Define and correctly use subjects and predicates when writing.

5. Define and correctly use complements when writing.

6. Define and correctly use modifiers when writing.

7. Describe and correctly use coordination when writing.

8. Describe and correctly use subordination when writing.

9. Identify and correctly use relative clauses when writing.

10. Define words.

11. Spell new words.

12. Write clear sentences.

Survey the LIFEPAC. Ask yourself some questions about this study and write your questions here.

_____
_____
_____
_____
_____
_____
_____
_____
_____
_____
_____
_____
_____
_____
_____
_____
_____
_____
_____

1. THE MECHANICS OF ENGLISH: PART I

In this section you will learn and review the correct usage of **capitalization**. Study this skill carefully. It will add much to your writing ability.

Spelling is also an important part of writing. Study the spelling lesson to increase your knowledge of spelling.

SECTION OBJECTIVES

Review these objectives. When you have completed this section, you should be able to:

1. Capitalize words correctly.
11. Spell new words.

VOCABULARY

Study these words to enhance your learning success in this section.

capitalize (kap′ u tu līz). Write or print with a capital letter, especially the first letter of a word.

direct quotation (du rekt′ kwō tā′ shun). Telling what a person said by using her exact words.

document (dok′ yu munt). Something written or printed that gives information or proves a fact.

modify (mod′ u fī). Change; limit the meaning of; adjectives modify nouns.

proper noun (prop′ ur noun). The name of a specific person, place, or thing; proper nouns are capitalized.

Note: *All vocabulary words in this LIFEPAC appear in* **boldface** *print the first time they are used. If you are not sure of the meaning when you are reading, study the definitions given.*

Pronunciation Key: h**a**t, **ā**ge, c**ã**re, f**ä**r; l**e**t, **ē**qual, t**ė**rm; **i**t, **ī**ce; h**o**t, **ō**pen, **ô**rder; **oi**l; **ou**t; c**u**p, p**u̇**t, r**ü**le; **ch**ild; lo**ng**; **th**in; /ŦH/ for **th**en; /zh/ for mea**s**ure; /u/ represents /a/ in **a**bout, /e/ in tak**e**n, /i/ in penc**i**l, /o/ in lem**o**n, and /u/ in circ**u**s.

CAPITAL LETTERS

How well can you write? Is your writing ability good, average, or poor? Would you like to improve your writing? Good writers know when to use capital letters; consequently, they also know when *not* to use capital letters. As you study the information in this section, be sure you understand when to use capital letters.

To help you understand when to use capital letters, the following rules will be studied.

1. **Capitalize** the first word of a sentence. Note: The word *capitalize* refers only to the first letter in a word.

Examples:

- *T*he weather is nice today.
- *D*o you like popcorn?

2. Capitalize the first word of a **direct quotation**.

Examples:

- And God said, "*L*et there be light"; and there was light.
- She answered, "*Y*es, I do."

3. Capitalize the first word of a line of poetry.

    Examples:

    ■ *I* wish I were a fish.
       *S*wimming in the sea.
       *D*on't you wish you were a bird
       *L*ooking from a tree?

4. Capitalize the names of people and products (**proper nouns**).

    Examples:

    ■ John, Mary Johnston, Clyde R. Ferguson

    ■ Coca Cola, Ajax, General Electric

    Do NOT capitalize: boy, girl, man, soda pop, cleanser, refrigerator

5. Capitalize words that refer to specific groups of people (proper adjectives).

    Examples: Canadians, Christian, Baptist

    Do NOT capitalize: people, religion, denomination

6. Capitalize geographical names (proper nouns).

    Examples: Elm Avenue, Phoenix, Minnesota, France, Atlantic Ocean, Rockies, Lake Michigan

    Do NOT capitalize: street, city, state, country, ocean, mountain, lake

7. Capitalize the names of schools, parks, buildings, organizations, and so forth (proper nouns).

    Examples: Friendship Christian School, Lincoln Park, Congress, Prince of Peace Church, Boy Scouts

    Do NOT capitalize: school, park, building, church, club

Capitalize all the words that need capitalizing by underlining the correct letter.
Refer to Rules 1 through 7 if you have questions.

1.1   whenever i hear the poem "the night before christmas," a special feeling comes over me. this year on december 23, my parents, john, cindy, and i are leaving for arizona to visit my grandparents. they live at 1655 north lincoln road in phoenix, arizona. on christmas eve we shall attend the special service at the first christian church. later, we shall return with my grandparents, mr. and mrs. simpson, to open gifts.

Underline all letters that should be capitalized, but are not capitalized.
Circle all letters that should not be capitalized but are.

Example: <u>w</u>e go to Ⓢchool near Ardmore park.

1.2   John said to ted, "please give me the wrench."

1.3   last summer we went to colorado and visited Denver, Vail, and two other Cities.

1.4   The scene I'd like to see

           is an elephant in a tree.

           He'd be looking for his kite

           wouldn't that be a sight?

1.5   Mary and She drank pepsi as they watched the Football game.

1.6   do you like french fried potatoes?

1.7   Have you ever seen the Pacific ocean?

1.8   My Family is from farmington, west Virginia.

1.9   Washington school is located on Main street.

1.10   Many of the members of our Church Youth Group are also members of the Philadelphia youth band.

1.11   My family attends Trinity Lutheran church.

8. Capitalize days of the week, months, holidays, and holy days (proper nouns).

   Examples: *W*ednesday, *A*pril, *L*abor *D*ay, *G*ood *F*riday

   Do NOT capitalize: day, month, holiday

9. Capitalize historical periods, events, dates, and **documents** (proper nouns).

   Examples: *R*enaissance, *K*orean *W*ar, *S*ummer of 1850, *D*eclaration of *I*ndependence, *J*uly 4, 1776

   Do NOT capitalize: summer, winter, spring, fall when used alone.

10. Capitalize personal titles (proper nouns).

    Examples: *M*ister Jones, *U*ncle Fred, *P*resident Jefferson, *P*rofessor Higgins, *Q*ueen Victoria, *P*astor Davis, *D*r. Thomas, *M*rs. Fields

    Do NOT capitalize: mother, father, uncle, aunt, doctor, or pastor when used in this way: I asked my mother . . . , I asked my doctor . . . , and so forth. Capitalize mother and father, when used as a name: I asked *M*other . . . , I told *F*ather . . . , and so on.

11. Capitalize the main words in titles.

    Examples: "Amazing Grace", "Song of Solomon", "Treasure Island"

12. The pronoun I is always capitalized (proper pronoun).

    Example: John and *I* are good friends.

13. Capitalize the Deity (God) and words which refer to God (proper nouns and personal pronouns).

    Examples: God, Father, Son, Holy Spirit, He, Him, His

14. Capitalize the names of languages (proper nouns and adjectives).

    Examples: *E*nglish, *F*rench, *S*panish, *C*hinese, *L*atin

15. Capitalize the names of school subjects with numbers after them (proper nouns).

    Examples: *A*lgebra 1, *R*eligion III, *F*rench, *E*nglish

    Do NOT capitalize: mathematics, history, art

Underline all letters that should be capitalized, but are not.
Circle all letters that should not be capitalized, but are.

1.12   The second friday in june is the last Day of school.

1.13   World war II was fought in the twentieth century.

1.14   The U.S. constitution is a blueprint of our Government.

1.15   I asked mother if my Father was home yet.

1.16   "The gift of the Magi" is my favorite short story.

1.17   Doreen and i frequently went swimming last Summer.

1.18   The holy trinity consists of God the father, the Son, and the Holy spirit.

1.19   Do You understand spanish?

1.20   My older brother is taking algebra 2, english, Wood Shop, History,

Physical Education, and religion at his high school.

1.21   Christmas is both a Holiday and a holy day.

Use correct capitalization in these activities.

1.22   Write a sentence that uses a direct quotation. _____

_____

1.23   Write a poem that has four lines.

_____

_____

_____

_____

1.24   Use the names of three people in a sentence. _____

_____

1.25   Use the names of three brands of potato chips in a sentence. _____

_____

1.26   Write a sentence that uses two words which refer to people (French, Christian, Roman, and

so forth). _____

_____

1.27   Write your full address, including street, city, state, and country.

_____

_____

_____

1.28   Write the name of an ocean, a mountain range, a lake, and a river.

_____   _____

_____   _____

1.29   Write the full name of your school. _____

_____

1.30   Write a sentence that uses a day of the week, a month, and the name of a holiday or holy

day. _____

_____

1.31   Write the names of an important document, historical period, and important event.

_____

_____

1.32   Write the titles and names of your pastor, principal, and teacher. _____

_____

1.33   Write a sentence using the word _mother_ or _father_ as a proper noun.

_____

1.34   Write the title of your favorite song. _____

_____

1.35   Write a sentence that refers to God. _____

_____

1.36   Write the names of three languages. _____

_____

Use capital letters wherever necessary in the following paragraphs.

1.37 vacationing this summer in the state of virginia, my family and i saw the blue ridge mountains. dad drove our camper through miles of back roads to reach the peaks of otter, a spectacular campground.

"wait for me," i shouted, as we raced for lake monroe.

"last one in washes the dishes," teased my older brother timothy, as he dashed ahead.

soon, we met a family from evanston, illinois who quickly became our friends. dr. miller had come to charlottesville to serve on the faculty at the university of virginia. the millers planned to stay in virginia through june, july, and august. their daughters, mary and linda, taught me to water ski.

together we spent many pleasant hours exploring the shenandoah valley. we saw the natural bridge, president woodrow wilson's home in staunton, and visited the campus of washington and lee in lexington. what impressed me most was general robert e. lee's horse, traveler, whose skeletal remains were perfectly preserved and enclosed in a glass showcase.

TEACHER CHECK _____ _____
                                   initials   date

Work this puzzle.

1.38 Crostic puzzles are fun to do, and they help a person to improve his or her vocabulary. In this LIFEPAC you will have one Bible crostic puzzle.*

Follow these directions.

> a. Begin at letter A.
>
> b. From each definition decide what the word should be and write it in the blank spaces opposite the definition. Put one letter in each space.
>
> c. Each space has a number under it. Transfer the letter you wrote in each space to the corresponding box with the same number over it at the other part of the puzzle.
>
> d. When you finish, you will have a familiar Bible quotation in the boxes.

A. God

$\overline{18}\ \overline{43}\ \overline{20}\ \overline{21}\ \overline{3}\ \overline{16}\ \overline{19}$

B. The place where God dwells

$\overline{4}\ \overline{5}\ \overline{30}\ \overline{31}\ \overline{7}\ \overline{10}$

C. Its square root is three or 3 x 3 = _____

$\overline{11}\ \overline{9}\ \overline{13}\ \overline{23}$

D. Four fingers and a thumb

$\overline{26}\ \overline{35}\ \overline{33}\ \overline{17}$

E. Under

$\overline{6}\ \overline{27}\ \overline{2}\ \overline{32}\ \overline{42}\ \overline{25}\ \overline{28}$

F. Not loose

$\overline{38}\ \overline{12}\ \overline{15}\ \overline{45}\ \overline{22}$

G. Short for Edward

$\overline{41}\ \overline{37}$

H. What you do with a shovel

$\overline{24}\ \overline{1}\ \overline{14}$

I. Receive

$\overline{8}\ \overline{29}\ \overline{44}$

J. Female chickens that lay eggs

$\overline{39}\ \overline{40}\ \overline{36}\ \overline{34}$

*Devised by Geraldine Jaffe

BIBLE CROSTIC PUZZLE

1	2	3	4	5	6	7	8	9	10	11	12	13	14	15	16	17
□	□	□	□	□	□	□	□	□	□	□	□	□	□	□	□	□

18	19	20	21	22	23	24	25	26	27	28	29	30	31	32	33	34
□	□	□	□	□	□	□	□	□	□	□	□	□	□	□	□	□

35	36	37	38	39	40	41	42	43	44	45
□	□	□	□	□	□	□	□	□	□	□

SPELLING

The spelling words in Spelling Words-1 are either adjectives or adverbs. Adjectives and adverbs are called modifiers. You will study modifiers later in this LIFEPAC. Some adverbs have endings that change the word from an adjective to an adverb.

Spelling Words-1		
quick*	finally**	quietly**
quickly**	slow*	backward***
careful*	slowly**	friendly***
carefully**	happy*	early***
extreme*	happier***	daily***
extremely**	happily**	somewhat**
angry*	quiet*	already**
final*	quieter***	fast***

The adjectives in Spelling Words-1 are followed by one asterisk, the adverbs by two. Those words with three asterisks can be used as either an adjective or an adverb.

Remember that in sentences, adjectives usually **modify** nouns (things), and adverbs modify verbs (actions).

 Write each spelling word in its appropriate column.

1.39

Adjectives	Adverbs	Adjective or Adverb
_____	_____	_____
_____	_____	_____
_____	_____	_____
_____	_____	_____
_____	_____	_____
_____	_____	_____
_____	_____	_____
_____	_____	

Answer this question.

1.40   What endings are on the adverbs in Spelling Words-1?

a. _____ and b. _____

Write sentences using words from Spelling Words-1.

1.41 Write three sentences using three different adjectives.

a. _____

b. _____

c. _____

1.42 Write three sentences using three different adverbs.

a. _____

b. _____

c. _____

1.43 Write three sentences using three different words that can be used as either adjectives or adverbs.

a. _____

b. _____

c. _____

ABC **Ask your teacher to give you a practice spelling test of Spelling Words-1.** Restudy the words you missed.

Review the material in this section in preparation for the Self Test. The Self Test will check your mastery of this particular section. The items missed on this Self Test will indicate specific areas where restudy is needed for mastery.

SELF TEST 1

Write true or false (each answer, 2 points).

1.01 _____ Proper nouns are always capitalized.

1.02 _____ The first word of a direct quotation is never capitalized.

1.03 _____ Words which refer to the Deity are seldom capitalized.

1.04 _____ The words *mother* and *father* are always capitalized.

1.05 _____ Always capitalize geographical names.

Match these items (each answer, 3 points).

1.06	_____ first word of a sentence	a.	capitalized
1.07	_____ first word of a direct quotation	b.	not capitalized
1.08	_____ first word of a line of poetry		
1.09	_____ all words in titles		
1.010	_____ all pronouns		

Match these items (each answer, 3 points).

1.011	_____ ajax, general electric	a.	capitalized
1.012	_____ mother, aunt, uncle	b.	not capitalized
1.013	_____ americans, methodists		
1.014	_____ first national bank		
1.015	_____ railroad park		
1.016	_____ mediterranean sea		
1.017	_____ denomination		

Underline all words that should be capitalized but are not. Circle all words that should not be capitalized but are (each answer, 1 point).

1.018 Bill said, "today is friday."

1.019 Our Family enjoys german food.

1.020 The Midville library is located near the Park on Elm avenue.

1.021 This Winter, father is going to buy us a sled.

1.022 Next year i'm going to study latin.

45 / 57   SCORE _____   TEACHER _____ _____
                                              initials   date

ABC **Take your spelling test of Spelling Words-1.**

2. THE MECHANICS OF ENGLISH: PART II

Section Two of this LIFEPAC deals with the correct usage of **punctuation**. In order to write in meaningful terms, learn specific rules about punctuation and then apply these rules to writing. Our first concern will be with the study of internal punctuation, specifically the apostrophe, quotation marks, parentheses, and the hyphen. A separate section will concentrate on the use of the comma in writing. The spelling list includes some of the punctuation terms and some words containing punctuation marks. Learning the definitions of the words is an important skill.

SECTION OBJECTIVES

Review these objectives. When you have completed this section, you should be able to:

2. Identify and correctly use the following internal punctuation: apostrophe, quotation marks, parentheses, and hyphen.

3. Explain the correct use of commas in introductory words and phrases, with coordinating conjunctions, with nonessential elements, and in series.

10. Define words.

11. Spell new words.

VOCABULARY

Study these words to enhance your learning success in this section.

clarity (klar′ u tē). Clearness.

compound (kom′ pound). Having more than one part; something made by combining parts.

confirm (kun fėrm′). Prove to be true or correct.

dialogue (dī′ u lôg). Conversation in a play, story, and so forth.

emphasis (em′ fu sis). Special force; importance.

indefinite pronoun (in def′ u nit prō′ noun). A pronoun such as *any, anyone, some,* and *somebody*.

indirect quotation (in du rekt′ kwō tā′ shun). Telling what a person said but not using his exact words.

introductory (in tru duk′ tur ē). Used to introduce.

nonessential (non u sen′ shul). Not essential; unimportant.

optional (op′ shu nul). Left to one's choice; not required.

parenthetic (par un thet′ ik). Characterized by adding an idea without changing the meaning.

plural (plür′ ul). Containing more than one.

possessive adjective (pu zes′ iv aj′ ik tiv). The form of an adjective that shows ownership such as, "the day's end."

possessive case (pu zes' iv kās). The form of a noun, pronoun, or adjective used to show ownership.

punctuation (pungk chu. ā' shun). The use of periods, commas, and other marks to help make the meaning clear.

set off (set of). Set apart; separate.

PUNCTUATION

When you speak to another person, you use your voice in special ways. Other than pronouncing words, you also use your voice to give **emphasis** and meaning to certain words and ideas. You give emphasis and meaning by pausing, by saying certain words louder or softer, and by changing the tone and pitch of your voice.

Although you cannot use your voice in special ways when you write, you have other tools you can use to give emphasis and meaning to words and ideas. In Section One you learned that we begin a sentence with a capital letter. This capital letter announces the beginning of a new idea. If the word "he" begins with a capital letter, it tells the reader that we are talking about God.

Punctuation is another tool we use to give meaning, emphasis, and **clarity** when we write. You are well aware of how to use periods and question marks at the ends of sentences. In particular, you know that a period at the end of a sentence marks the end of an idea or thought. This kind of punctuation is called *outside punctuation,* because it comes at the end of a sentence.

Punctuation that occurs within a sentence is called *inside or internal punctuation*. In addition to quotation marks and parentheses, inside punctuation includes the apostrophe, hyphen, and comma. You will now study the special ways these punctuation marks are used.

The apostrophe. The apostrophe is used to form the **possessive case** of nouns and **indefinite pronouns**.

The possessive case of *personal pronouns* does not require the use of an apostrophe.

Example: 1.

■ *my* coat (*My* shows possession or ownership of *coat*.)

■ *his* coat

■ *your* coat

■ Also: her, our, their, its, whose

Example: 2.

■ That coat is *hers.*

■ That coat is *yours.*

■ Also: mine, ours, theirs

The possessive case of *indefinite pronouns* is formed by adding *'s*.

Examples:

■ anyone's coat (*Anyone's* shows possession or ownership of *coat*.)

■ somebody's coat

■ Also: one, everyone, everybody, no one, nobody, anybody, someone

The possessive case of *singular nouns* is formed by adding *'s*.

Examples:

■ man's coat (*Man's* shows possession or ownership of *coat*.)

■ Jane's coat

■ mother's coat

The possessive case of **plural** nouns not ending in *s* is formed by adding 's.

Examples:

- children's coats
- men's coats

The possessive case of plural nouns that end with *s* is formed by adding an apostrophe (') after the *s*.

Examples:

- ladies' coats
- boys' coats

Certain **possessive adjectives** require 's.

Examples:

- a month's subscription
- this morning's breakfast
- a dollar's worth

 Use the apostrophe to form the possessive case of the nouns and underline all the personal pronouns.

2.1   Jims bicycle is missing, and his paper routes collections have also disappeared.

2.2   The voters duty is to appear at his districts polls on Tuesday.

2.3   Freshmens textbooks are always the last to be distributed.

2.4   Mothers cakes never remain in her kitchen very long.

2.5   You get your dollars worth at the discount stores sale.

When two or more words are used to show joint possession or ownership, only the last word is possessive.

Examples:

- John and Bill's boat. (The boat belongs to both John and Bill.)
- Jill, Sue, and Brenda's ball

- Jackson and Johnson's Hardware Store

When two or more persons possess or own items individually, each name is in possessive case.

Example: John's and Bill's coats (John and Bill each own a coat.)

Place an apostrophe (') or 's wherever needed.

2.6   somebody   pencil

2.7   Bob   skates

2.8   the two boys   ball

2.9   sheep   wool

2.10   a week   vacation

2.11   Bob   and Mary   houses

2.12   Smith and West   Pharmacy

2.13   women   cakes

2.14   a dollar   worth of candy

2.15   Sandy and Regina   radio

2.16   no one   fault

2.17   the three chairs   legs

2.18   Fred, Frank, and Harry   basketball

2.19   mother   car

The apostrophe (') is used to show which letters are omitted in a contraction.

■ *Note*: A contraction is two words joined to make one. An apostrophe is substituted for one or more of the letters which are dropped.

When a word joins *not* to make a contraction, drop the *o* and replace it with an apostrophe.

Examples:

■ could + n*o*t = couldn't

■ is + n*o*t = isn't

In other contractions the apostrophe usually replaces the first part of the second word.

Examples:

■ could h*a*ve = could've

■ I *a*m = I'm

 Write a contraction for each of the following expressions:

2.20 cannot _____

2.21 do not _____

2.22 he will _____

2.23 I will _____

2.24 it is _____

2.25 she would _____

2.26 should not _____

2.27 they are _____

2.28 we are _____

2.29 will not _____

The apostrophe is also used to form the plurals of letters and figures.

Examples:

■ a. Be sure to cross your *t*'s and dot your *i*'s.

■ b. His 8's are hard to read.

 Use the apostrophe correctly.

2.30 Write a sentence that uses the possessive case of an indefinite pronoun.

_____

2.31 Write a sentence that uses the possessive case of a singular noun.

_____

_____

2.32 Write a sentence that uses the possessive case of a plural noun that *does not* end in *s*.

_____

_____

2.33   Write a sentence that uses the possessive case of a plural noun that does end with *s*.

_____

_____

2.34   Write a sentence that shows two or more names having joint ownership of a boat.

_____

_____

2.35   Write a sentence that shows two or more names having individual ownership of pencils.

_____

_____

2.36   Write a sentence containing two contractions. _____

_____

2.37   Write a sentence that uses the plural form of a letter or figure. _____

_____

Put in apostrophes where necessary. Refer to your rules if you are not sure.

2.38   Ive just read todays paper. Its just amazing how much of it is composed of advertisements. My mothers first move is to scan the papers pages for ladies sales. My fathers preference is the editorial section; he diligently reads the editors columns. Hes especially interested in readers comments and their reactions. Im a sports fan, myself. Doesnt the World Series brand of baseball appeal to you? I cant imagine anyones refusing to follow sports; but, then, neither can I imagine someones being interested in the days sales specials.

TEACHER CHECK _____ _____
                                    initials   date

Quotation marks (" ___ "). Quotation marks are used to indicate direct quotations and **dialogue**.

Use quotation marks at the beginning and at the end of a direct quotation (the words a person said).

Example: Helen said, "I am going to church."

Do not use quotation marks for an **indirect quotation**.

Example: Helen said that she was going to church.

Begin a direct quotation with a capital letter if it is a complete sentence.

Examples:

■ Manuel said, "*It* is going to rain."

■ Rita asked, "*How* do you know?"

■ "*I* heard it on the radio," he answered.

When a direct quotation is broken into two parts, do not begin the second part with a capital letter unless it is a new sentence. Each part has its own quotation marks.

Example:

■ "Though you don't know how to ski," replied Maria, "you can go on the snow trip with the rest of the group." "I enjoy reading books," Mac said. "They are like good friends."

Use a comma to separate a direct quotation from the rest of the sentence.

Place commas and periods inside quotation marks.

Example: "I wish I could go," he said, "but it's not possible."

Place question marks and exclamation points inside quotation marks if the quotation is a question or exclamation.

Examples:

■ Marnie asked, "Are you happy?"

■ "Yes, I am!" shouted Kenney.

When writing dialogue, start a new paragraph each time the speaker changes.

Example:

■ "My uncle has a boat, and he took my cousin and me to the lake."
"Does your cousin know how to water ski?"
"Yes, she's very good at it. She was the one who taught me how to water ski. You ought to try it some time."

 Place quotation marks where needed.

2.39   Brent said, It is getting late.

2.40   Today is Friday, said Mary Lou, and we have a three day vacation from school.

2.41   Have you ever seen an alligator? asked Wendy.

2.42   I can't go with you, said Fred. Thank you for asking me.

2.43   When I was your age, my father said, I had to walk seven miles in the snow to get to school, and it was uphill both ways!

Quotation marks are used for certain titles.

Use quotation marks for the titles of short stories, songs, and poems.

Examples:

■ Robert Frost's "The Pasture"

■ Bret Harte's "The Outcast of Poker Flat"

■ The children's song, "Mary Had a Little Lamb"

Use quotation marks for the titles of book chapters.

Example: The title of Chapter 7 in this history book is "The Westward Movement."

Use quotation marks for the titles of newspaper and magazine articles.

Examples:

■ I read an article in the *Times* entitled, "The President Goes to China."

■ Did you see the article in the *Reader's Digest* called, "How to Live a Healthy Life"?

Use quotation marks for the titles of special programs.

Examples:

■ "The Paul Harvey News"

■ "The Old Fashioned Revival Hour"

Use quotation marks for words used in a special or unusual way.

Examples:

■ She calls herself "queen," but she is just like anyone else.

■ The word, "pseudonym", is hard to spell.

 Place quotation marks where needed.

2.44   He read a poem entitled, The Prayer of the Little Bird.

2.45   Are you familiar with Hans Christian Andersen's The Emperor's New Clothes?

2.46   His favorite hymn is Onward, Christian Soldiers.

2.47   Did you read the article, Human Rights on Trial in *Time* Magazine?

2.48   I listened to The Six O'Clock News on station KFLR.

2.49   She is as sweet as lemon juice.

2.50   That is really hot.

Use quotation marks correctly.

2.51   Write a sentence that contains a direct quotation. _____

_____

2.52   Write a sentence that uses an indirect quotation. _____

_____

2.53   Write a sentence with a direct quotation that is broken into two parts.

_____

_____

2.54 Write a brief dialogue between two people. _____

_____

_____

_____

_____

2.55 Write the title of your favorite poem. _____

_____

2.56 Write the title of your favorite short story. _____

_____

2.57 Write the title of this section of Language Arts LIFEPAC 706. _____

_____

2.58 Write the title of your favorite song. _____

_____

2.59 Write the title of a magazine article. _____

_____

2.60 Write a sentence that uses a word in a special or unusual way. _____

_____

Test your ability to use quotation marks and marks of punctuation used within quotation marks. Remember the rule to begin a new paragraph each time the speaker changes. Indicate paragraph change with this symbol (L).

2.61 Can you remember the thrill of your first airplane ride? asked Mark. Yes, replied Chris as he took another bite out of an apple. What a sensation to feel yourself lifting off the ground, he exclaimed, or is it a sensation of the earth falling away? Anyway, what part of flying do you enjoy most? The meals! Andy contributed, as he bit into another apple. On the trip to San Diego, we had steak, potatoes, broccoli, salad, rolls, and chocolate cake. Obviously, replied Mark, your big thrill was the menu. What I like about flying is to see how small everything appears back on the ground, said Chris. For instance, roads and rivers look like ribbons. Yeah, interrupted Mark, and lakes look like puddles and cars look like ants. Speaking of flying, said Andy, we are all late for history class.

TEACHER CHECK _____ _____

                                    initials   date

Parentheses. Use parentheses to enclose **parenthetic**, supplementary, and explanatory material.

Note: A parenthetic expression is a group of words, an idea, that is not closely related to the rest of the sentence. Supplementary material would be an added idea. It is somewhat similar to a parenthetic expression. Explanatory ideas give an extra explanation to help the reader better understand the main idea of a sentence. Information enclosed in parentheses does not change the meaning of the sentence. We use parentheses when the idea that interrupts the main part of the sentence is very noticeable. If the interruption is less noticeable, we usually use commas instead. Parentheses enclose parenthetic expressions.

Example: The old radios *(none of them work)* are being donated to the rummage sale.

Parentheses enclose supplementary material.

Example: He is hoping *(as we all are)* that he does well in school this year.

Parentheses enclose (surround) explanatory material (ideas).

Note: Look again at the last sentence. The words, *surround* and *ideas,* are enclosed in parentheses because they explain the word that comes before each. They tell us that *enclose* means *surround,* and *material* means *ideas.*

Use parentheses to enclose numerical figures (numbers) which **confirm** a written number.

Example: The cost of thirty *(30)* packages of papers is fifty dollars *($50)*.

Note: The use of parentheses in this way is frequently used in business. It is seldom used in other kinds of writing.

Use parentheses to enclose numbers or letters in a series.

Example: A good student always brings the following items to class: his *(1)* book, *(2)* paper, *(3)* pens, and *(4)* pencils.

Note: If a *list* of ideas or words is used, the use of parentheses is **optional**.

The hyphen (-). Use a hyphen to divide a word at the end of a line that is to be carried over to the next line.

Divide words between syllables.

Examples:

- **Incorrect**: We ate dinner with our grand parents.

- **Correct**: We ate dinner with our grand-parents.

Note: Check your dictionary if you are not sure of a word's syllables.

Never divide a one-syllable word.

Examples:

- **Incorrect**: We like to feed bread *cru-mbs* to birds.

- **Correct**: We like to feed bread *crumbs* to birds.

Divide words evenly.

Examples:

- **Awkward**: He told me he was *in-terested* in model airplanes.

- **Correct**: He told me he was *inter-ested* in model airplanes.

When writing formal English, do not divide capitalized words.

Examples:

- **Incorrect**: This year we studied *Amer-ican* history.

- **Correct**: This year we studied *American* history.

Use a hyphen to separate the parts of compound numbers from twenty-one to ninety-nine when they are written in words.

Examples:

- *thirty-two* students

- *twenty-one* years old

- *seventy-five* cents

Use a hyphen to separate fractions written in words that are used as adjectives.

Examples:

- a three-fourths majority

- *but*, three fourths of the people

Use a hyphen to separate a prefix from a proper noun or adjective.

Examples: un-American, pre-Christian, anti-Russian

Use a hyphen to separate the prefixes *all-*, *self-*, and *ex-* when they are added to nouns.

Examples: all-star, ex-president, self-regard

Use a hyphen to separate certain compound words.

Examples: secretary-treasurer, mother-in-law, president-elect, day-to-day

 Use hyphens correctly.

2.62   Write a sentence showing how you would divide a word at the end of a line.

_____

_____

2.63   Write the numbers 28, 47, and 65 as words. _____

_____

2.64   Write a sentence that uses a fraction written in words as an adjective. _____

_____

2.65   Write a sentence that uses a proper noun with a prefix. _____

_____

2.66   Write a sentence with a word that combines the prefix *all-*, *ex-*, or *self-* with a noun.

_____

_____

2.67   Write a sentence using the words *brother-in-law*. _____

_____

COMMAS

Commas have an important function to perform in writing. Without commas, readers would be unable to properly interpret the writer's ideas. To avoid confusion, commas serve as signals that give meaning and clarity to sentences.

Use a comma after **introductory** words and phrases. Names of people used in direct address are separated from the rest of the sentence with a comma.

Examples:

- *Fred*, please come here.

Also: Please come here, *Fred*.

- If you do this job for me, *Bill*, I'll pay you five dollars.

The words *yes, no, why,* and *well* are followed by a comma when they are used as the first word of a sentence.

Examples:

- Yes, you may go.
- No, I don't like fishing.
- Well, if that's the way you want it.
- Why, you've spent all your money!

Note: A main, or independent clause, has a subject and a verb. It expresses a complete idea and can stand alone as a sentence. A subordinate, or dependent clause, expresses an idea or gives added information, but it cannot stand alone as a sentence. When a subordinate clause is placed before an independent clause, put a comma after the subordinate clause.

Many introductory phrases and clauses are followed by a comma.

Examples:

- *After Sue washed her hair,* she borrowed her mother's hair drier.
- *By the end of the day*, Father was very tired.
- *Writing as fast as she could*, our class secretary tried her best to take notes.

Most *short* introductory phrases do *not* require a comma.

Examples:

- *Before today* he had never eaten snails.
- *In the future* I will go to college.

When a modifier such as an adjective, an adverb, or a participle is used as an introductory word, it should be followed by a comma.

Examples:

- *Happy and warm*, the baby quickly fell asleep.
- *Excitedly*, Fran screamed and cheered.
- *Coughing*, the engine came to life.
- *Annoyed,* the children began to complain.

 Place commas where necessary.

2.68 Mary please wash the dishes.

2.69 Yes I like to play tennis.

2.70 Before she cooked the breakfast Mother read her Bible.

2.71 Near the end of the first week we had earned enough money for our camping trip.

2.72 Sliding into third base David tries to avoid the tag.

2.73 During lunch he took a nap.

2.74 Quietly Sandy tiptoed out of the room.

2.75 Sad and discouraged Julia wanted to be alone.

or nor and but for

Use a comma before coordinating conjunctions when they join independent clauses.

As you know, an independent clause contains a subject and a verb. It can stand alone as a sentence. Observe two examples of independent clauses: (1) <u>Today</u> <u><u>is</u></u> warm. (2) <u>Yesterday</u> <u><u>was</u></u> cold. In each example, the subject is underlined once and the verb is underlined twice. Each example is a complete sentence.

Two independent clauses can be joined to make one sentence. A sentence with two independent clauses is a **compound** *sentence*. When independent clauses are joined, they must have a comma and a coordinating conjunction between them. The most common coordinating conjunctions are these: *and, but, or, nor,* and *for*.

Examples:

- I like lemonade, *and* Bill likes orange juice.
- Todd must clean the windows, *or* his parents will be very angry.

If the independent clauses are very short, a comma is not necessary before the coordinating conjunction.

Examples:

- I am able *but* you are not.
- You can go *or* you can stay.

When a group of words has a verb but no subject, it is a phrase. A comma is not used when a phrase comes after an independent clause.

Examples:

- I read the chapter *and* answered the questions.
- John will play chess *or* read a book.

When a coordinating conjunction simply joins two words or phrases, do not use a comma.

Examples:

- bread *and* butter
- He has a strong body *and* a weak mind.

 Place commas where necessary. Some sentences will not have commas.

2.76   Dogs are nice but you must take good care of them.

2.77   Bill must study for his test or he will not get a good grade.

2.78   I have to go for it is late.

2.79   Janice read the Bible and said her prayers.

2.80   She has five dollars and thirty-five cents.

Use commas to set off **nonessential** elements.

Use commas before and after an idea that interrupts a sentence.

You may remember that if the interruption is very noticeable, you use parentheses. If the interruption is less noticeable, you use commas instead.

Example: Mildred, *of course*, does not approve of spitting.

Use only one comma if an interruption comes at the beginning or end of a sentence:

Examples:

■ *Of course*, Mildred does not approve of spitting.

■ Mildred does not approve of spitting, *of course*.

Use commas to **set off** parenthetic words, phrases, and clauses.

A parenthetic expression will not change the meaning of a sentence; therefore, the meaning of the sentence will not change if the parenthetic expression is left out.

Examples:

■ I told him, *if you must know*, that I did not care for his behavior.

■ *Generally speaking*, the sky is blue.

■ It is the thought that is important, *not the gift*.

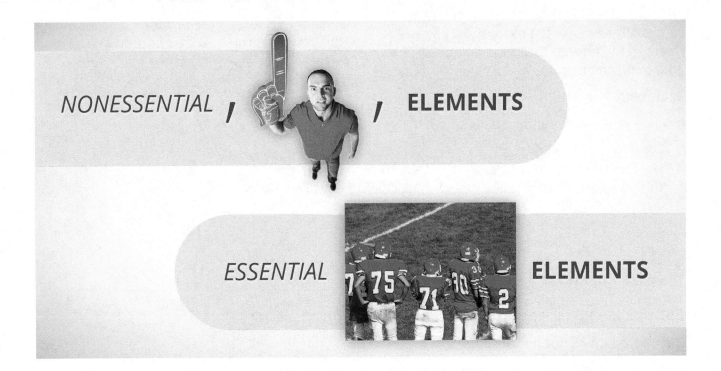

NONESSENTIAL , ELEMENTS

ESSENTIAL ELEMENTS

Write true or false.

2.81 _____ A comma is not used after long introductory phrases.

2.82 _____ Two independent clauses joined by a conjunction have a comma before the conjunction.

2.83 _____ A parenthetic expression changes the meaning of a sentence.

2.84 _____ Two words or phrases joined by a coordinating conjunction do not require a comma.

2.85 _____ An independent clause contains both a subject and a verb.

2.86 _____ Short introductory phrases require a comma.

2.87 _____ Commas are used to set off nonessential elements.

Use commas to set off appositives and their modifiers.

An appositive is a word, or group of words, that comes after a noun or pronoun. An appositive refers to the noun or pronoun and often gives added information.

Examples:

■ Mrs. Jones, *our librarian*, helped me find a book.

■ Ron, *the tallest boy in our class*, is the captain of the basketball team.

■ My grandfather, *a minister*, is now retired.

■ My favorite sport, *bowling*, is costly.

Go back and reread the last four sentences. This time, skip the italicized portion of each sentence. Does each sentence make sense?

When an appositive is closely related to the word before it, do not use a comma.

Examples:

■ Uncle John

■ my sister Jane

 Use commas to punctuate these sentences.

2.88 Cold and wet we rushed to warm ourselves around the fire.

2.89 No we will not be able to go.

2.90 After I finish my homework I will watch the high school football game.

2.91 Mark likes to play tennis and I like to play soccer.

2.92 Bob likes to play football of course.

2.93 John the captain of our football team dislocated his shoulder.

2.94 When we board the bus Frank looks for a seat by a window.

Use commas to set off nonrestrictive clauses.

A nonrestrictive clause is usually used as an adjective. It modifies a noun. A nonrestrictive clause adds information to a sentence, but it doesn't change the meaning.

Examples:

- William Philleo, *who is my friend*, helped me build a go-kart.
- Last Wednesday, *which was the Fourth of July*, we had a picnic.

As you did before, go back and read the last two sentences again, skipping the italicized portions. The meaning of each sentence does not change.

A restrictive clause is also used as an adjective, but it is essential to the meaning of a sentence. Restrictive clauses are *not* set off with commas.

Examples:

- The man *who arrived yesterday* was my Uncle David.
- The dress *that she is wearing* is nice.
- The car *that is parked in front of our house* is new.

If you were to read the last three sentences again and skip the italicized portions, some of the meaning would be lost in each sentence.

Use commas to set off nonrestrictive phrases.

A nonrestrictive phrase is used as an adjective. It adds information, but it is not essential to the meaning of the sentence.

Example: Brenda, *wishing to be finished*, started to work faster.

Read the sentence again, skipping the italicized portion. As before, the meaning of the sentence does not change.

A participial phrase that is necessary to the meaning of a sentence is restrictive and is not set off with commas.

Example: People *wishing to be finished* should work faster.

If you were to skip the italicized portion in the last sentence, some of the meaning would be lost.

Use commas to set off absolute phrases.

An absolute phrase is a group of words that has no grammatical relationship to any other word in a sentence.

Examples:

- *The hour being late,* we adjourned the meeting until tomorrow.
- I swam by myself, *my friends having gone to the game.*

Note: Do not be too concerned with grammatical terms such as participial phrase, absolute phrase, appositives, and so forth. You need to remember only two ideas:

1. If a word, a phrase, or a clause is not essential to the meaning of a sentence or if it simply adds more information without changing the meaning of a sentence, set the material off with commas.

2. If a word, phrase, or clause is essential to the meaning of a sentence, do not set it off with commas.

Place commas where necessary. Some sentences will not have commas.

2.95   Richard on the other hand does not enjoy ice skating.

2.96   By and large most teenage boys are big eaters.

2.97   Dr. Williams a dentist is very skillful.

2.98   My brother Danny is very strong.

2.99   Mrs. Sullivan who is my piano teacher has thirty students.

2.100   The teacher who teaches piano was ill last week and canceled all lessons.

Use commas to separate words, phrases, or clauses in a series.

A series is three or more items that come one after another in a sentence.

Examples:

■ blue, red, and yellow

■ For lunch, Jerry had two sandwiches, an apple, and a glass of milk.

■ I don't know if I should do my homework, take a nap, or play with my friends.

When the conjunction *and* comes before the last item in a series, it is correct to use a comma before the conjunction.

Example: She likes apples, oranges, peaches, and plums.

It is also correct to *not* use a comma before the conjunction *and*.

Example: She likes apples, oranges, peaches and plums. (no comma)

Note: Confusion is sometimes avoided by using a comma before the conjunction.

Ask your teacher whether you should use a comma before the conjunction *and*. Be consistent in the method you use.

Do not use commas if all the items in a series are separated by a conjunction.

Examples:

■ We visited Boston and New York and Philadelphia.

■ Bob or Jose or Hans will be our representative.

 Place commas where necessary. Some commas will be optional. Some sentences will not have commas.

2.101   We ate ice cream cake and candy.

2.102   Josephine Alice and Julaine will correct the tests.

2.103   We saw bears and snakes and lions at the zoo.

2.104   I brushed my teeth cleaned my nails and combed my hair.

2.105   We will paint the room white or yellow or light blue.

2.106   We went to the store and bought meat vegetables fruit bread canned goods milk eggs and sugar.

Use a comma to separate the day from the year in a date.

Example: May 15, 1995

When a date appears in the middle of a sentence, a comma is placed after the year.

Example: On May 15, 1995, our class will go on a nature hike.

Use a comma to separate the city from a state.

Example: Portland, Oregon

When a city and state appear in the middle of a sentence, a comma is placed after the state.

Example: Our family visited Portland, Oregon, last year.

Use commas where necessary. Refer to the rules if you are not certain.

2.107 My favorite ice creams are strawberry chocolate butter pecan and peppermint.

2.108 Ted answer the phone please.

2.109 Dr. Warren our family dentist lives across the street.

2.110 On May 6 1995 I moved to St. Louis Missouri.

2.111 That information in my opinion is totally incorrect.

2.112 Yes I bought fruit cookies lettuce and bread in the grocery store.

2.113 Uncle Jack the man in the blue suit is a college professor.

2.114 We ran the first three miles but we walked the last two miles to the beach.

2.115 Tommy my little brother can read write add subtract and multiply.

2.116 On the way home we found the road to be rocky narrow and dangerous.

Use commas correctly.

2.117 Write a sentence beginning with the name of a person used in direct address.

_____

2.118 Write the same sentence two more times: once with the person's name at the end of the sentence and again with the person's name in the middle of the sentence.

_____

_____

2.119 Write a sentence beginning with the word *yes*. _____

_____

2.120 Write a sentence beginning with the word *well*. _____

_____

2.121 Write a sentence that begins with a phrase and ends with an independent clause.

_____

_____

2.122 Write a sentence that begins with two adjectives, such as "cold and wet."

_____

2.123 Write a sentence that begins with an adverb such as "angrily". _____

_____

2.124 Write a sentence that combines these two independent clauses: (1) the water is cold (2) the sand is warm. _____

_____

2.125 Write a sentence that combines the following independent clause and phrase: (1) Jean painted with watercolors (2) listened to the music.

_____

2.126 Write a sentence that uses the phrase, "on the other hand," in the middle of it.

_____

_____

2.127 Write a sentence that ends with the parenthetic expression, "generally speaking."

_____

_____

2.128 Write a sentence with an appositive. _____

_____

_____

2.129 Write a sentence containing a restrictive clause. _____

_____

_____

2.130 Write a sentence containing a nonrestrictive clause. _____

_____

_____

2.131 Write a sentence that has a nonrestrictive phrase. _____

_____

_____

Select the correct punctuation rule and write it in the blanks.

2.132 For each item write *A* for apostrophe, *C* for comma, *H* for hyphen, *P* for parentheses, and *QM* for quotation marks.

a. _____ used with letter *s* to form the possessive case of singular nouns

b. _____ used with titles of songs and short stories

c. _____ used to separate words in series

d. _____ used to join compound numbers and words

e. _____ used with an idea that interrupts a sentence and is very noticeable

f. _____ used to set off nonrestrictive clauses and phrases

Your study of commas in this section will be important to you when you study *coordination* and *subordination* in the fourth section. You may want to look at this information again when you are studying those topics.

Write a biography. When you were working with Language Arts LIFEPAC 703, one of your assignments was to write a two- or three-page biography about one of your grandparents. You will now have a chance to write a two- or three-page biography about another grandparent.

2.133 Check the box as you complete each step in this activity. Use a separate piece of paper.

☐ Interview one of your parents about a grandparent's life story. If the grandparent you are going to write about is still alive, you may wish to interview him or her rather than one of your parents.

☐ Make a list of the sequence of events in this person's life. Limit the number of events to between four and six.

☐ Begin with when and where this person was born and tell something about his childhood.

☐ If possible, include an interesting experience this person had sometime in his life.

☐ Refer to your list and write an introductory paragraph about the subject of your biography.

☐ Write one paragraph about each event in your list.

☐ Write an ending paragraph that tells the most important thing to remember about your grandparent (no new information).

☐ Use a variety of proper nouns and adjectives.

☐ Write sentences that require different kinds of punctuation. This assignment should give you an opportunity to use commas, apostrophes, hyphens, quotation marks, and parentheses.

☐ Be sure you use correct grammar, spelling, usage, capitalization, and punctuation before you show your work to your teacher.

TEACHER CHECK _____ _____

initials   date

SPELLING

This spelling lesson contains several types of words. Some words are hyphenated, some are possessive forms, some are contractions, and others are proper nouns. These words are quite simple to spell, yet they may be tricky.

Spelling Words-2		
Tuesday	I'm	Chinese
yours	seventy-four	nonrestrictive
everyone	Christian	un-American
Canadian	theirs	Wednesday
man's	all-star	mother-in-law
parenthetic	February	children's
they're	nonessential	December
Pacific Ocean	ladies'	couldn't
no one		

Complete these activities.

2.134 Write a sentence illustrating the meaning of each word.

a. man's _____

b. parenthetic _____

c. they're _____

d. Pacific Ocean _____

e. I'm _____

f. seventy-four _____

g. all-star _____

h. February _____

i. no one _____

j. Chinese _____

k. un-American _____

l. Wednesday _____

m. mother-in-law _____

n. couldn't _____

2.135 Work this puzzle.

Across

1. a believer
2. not limiting
6. month of Christ's birth
8. contraction
9. women (poss.)
10. belonging to one male
11. not ours

Down

1. our neighbor to the north
3. a school day
4. not parents'
5. all
7. an Asian people

ABC Ask your teacher to give you a practice spelling test of Spelling Words-2. Restudy the words you missed.

↺ **Review the material in this section in preparation for the Self Test.** The Self Test will check your mastery of this particular section as well as your knowledge of the previous section. The items missed on this Self Test will indicate specific areas where restudy is needed for mastery.

SELF TEST 2

Write true or false (each answer, 1 point).

2.01 _____ All proper nouns, pronouns, and adjectives are capitalized.

2.02 _____ The first word in a sentence, in a direct quotation, and in a line of poetry is capitalized.

2.03 _____ The possessive case of personal pronouns requires the use of an apostrophe.

2.04 _____ Quotation marks are used for both direct and indirect quotations.

2.05 _____ A parenthetic expression is a nonessential element because it doesn't change the meaning of a sentence.

For each item write *A* for apostrophe, *C* for comma, *H* for hyphen, *P* for parentheses, and *QM* for quotation marks (each answer, 3 points).

2.06 _____ used to show the exact words a person said

2.07 _____ used after an introductory word or phrase

2.08 _____ used with letter *s* to form the possessive case of singular nouns

2.09 _____ used to join compound numbers and words

2.010 _____ used to set off nonrestrictive clauses and phrases

2.011 _____ used to enclose numerical figures which confirm a written number

2.012 _____ used with titles of songs and short stories

2.013 _____ used to show what letters were dropped in a contraction

2.014 _____ used to join written-out fractions that are adjectives

2.015 _____ used with an idea that interrupts a sentence and is very noticeable

Underline all words that should be capitalized but are not.
Circle all words that should not be but are (each answer, 1 point).

2.016 The martins just returned from sweden.

2.017 The Government is attempting to make Reforms.

2.018 In the Summer, we will vacation at lake powell.

2.019 This Semester, I'm taking math, History, latin and english.

2.020 The library of congress is located in washington.

Add the correct punctuation marks where needed (each numbered item, 4 points).

2.021 Mother said Mary please come here.

2.022 My mothers new outfit its blue is pretty.

2.023 This evenings dinner will consist of soup salad a main course and a dessert.

2.024 Before Carl answered the telephone he closed the door.

2.025 Slowly and deliberately Sandy stated that she hopes as we all do that Nancy will come to know Jesus.

2.026 You can come with us or you can stay at your uncles house.

2.027 Generally speaking the ladies Bible study lasts forty-five minutes.

2.028 If you want to go with us said Jack you must be at my house on time.

2.029 Our pastor a man of much learning attended Yale Divinity School.

2.030 Yes we all sang The Star Spangled Banner.

Write sentences using the following words (each answer, 4 points).

2.031 clarity _____

2.032 dialogue _____

2.033 document _____

2.034 optional _____

2.035 plural _____

80/100   **SCORE**_____   **TEACHER**_____ _____
                                                    initials   date

ABC **Take your spelling test of Spelling Words-2.**

LANGUAGE ARTS 706

LIFEPAC TEST

NAME _____

DATE _____

SCORE _____

LANGUAGE ARTS 706: LIFEPAC TEST

Answer true or false (each answer, 2 points).

1. _____ The first word of a line of poetry is capitalized.

2. _____ Periods and question marks are examples of "inside punctuation."

3. _____ Nonrestrictive clauses are not set off with commas.

4. _____ Either the complete subject or the complete predicate in a sentence can have an adjective.

5. _____ The words *a, an*, and *the* are adverbs.

6. _____ Coordination requires a minimum of three words.

7. _____ Nouns, proper nouns, and personal pronouns cannot be mixed when using coordination.

8. _____ In subordination, a less important idea will not usually change the meaning of a more important idea.

9. _____ A subordinate clause begins with a subordinating conjunction when a relationship is to be shown.

10. _____ A relative clause is a subordinate clause.

For each statement, write *A* for apostrophe, *C* for comma, *H* for hyphen, *P* for parentheses, or *QM* for quotation marks (each answer, 3 points).

11. _____ Used with titles of songs and short stories.

12. _____ Used to enclose numerical figures which confirm a written number.

13. _____ Used with letter *s* to form the possessive case of singular nouns.

14. _____ Used after an introductory word or phrase.

15. _____ Used to separate fractions written in words that are adjectives.

Write the letter or letters before the word or words that should be capitalized (each numbered problem, 3 points).

16. _____ a. man   b. cola   c. john r. smith   d. to father

17. _____ a. happy   b. old   c. french   d. protestant

18. _____ a. oak street   b. elm tree   c. ocean   d. arkansas

19. _____ a. month   b. labor day   c. good Friday   d. war

20. _____ a. aunt Martha b. cousin   c. mrs.   d. professor Smith

Underline adjectives once, adverbs twice, and prepositional phrases three times (each sentence, 3 points).

21. The old man jumped up and down.

22. Mother put beans in the jar.

23. I am happy.

24. She is very happy.

25. To spit on the sidewalk is not nice.

Write *compound* or *complex* to indicate whether each sentence is a compound sentence or a complex sentence (each answer, 4 points).

26. Jesus is my Savior, and He died for my sins. _____

27. Because Jan has a good personality, she has many friends. _____

28. I will see you after I return from Omaha. _____

29. We will go or we will stay. _____

30. The weather is turning colder; in fact, it may snow tomorrow. _____

Write *time*, *place*, *cause*, or *requirement* to show the relationship that exists in each subordinate sentence (each answer, 4 points).

31. Wherever you go, you can see the sun. _____

32. Before he left, Father locked the door. _____

33. I won't go unless it is necessary. _____

34. Because she is new, Jill doesn't know many people. _____

ABC **Take your LIFEPAC Spelling Test.**

3. THE STRUCTURE OF ENGLISH: PART I

A simple sentence is defined as a group of words that contains a **subject** and a **predicate** and that expresses a complete thought. Sentences sometimes also contain a **complement**—a word in the predicate that modifies, explains, or completes the meaning of either the subject or the predicate. For clearer and more precise meanings, sentences also usually contain modifiers. In this section of Language Arts LIFEPAC 706, you will study subjects and predicates, complements, and modifiers.

SECTION OBJECTIVES

Review these objectives. When you have completed this section, you should be able to:

4.   Define and correctly use subjects and predicates when writing.

5.   Define and correctly use complements when writing.

6.   Define and correctly use modifiers when writing.

VOCABULARY

Study these words to enhance your learning success in this section.

complement (kom′ plu munt). A word or group of words that completes the meaning of either the subject or the predicate.

core (kôr). The central or most important part.

direct object (du rekt′ ob′ jikt). Words that tell who or what undergoes the action of the verb.

indirect object (in′ du rekt′ ob′ jikt). Words that tell who or what is indirectly affected by the action of the verb.

predicate (pred′ u kit). The words expressing what is said about the subject.

predicate adjective (pred′ u kit aj′ ik tiv). An adjective in the predicate that describes the subject.

predicate nominative (pred′ u kit nom′ u nu tiv). A noun or pronoun in the predicate that refers to the subject.

preposition (prep′ u zish′ un). A word that joins a noun or a pronoun to some other word in the sentence.

subject (sub′ jikt). The words that tell who or what the sentence is about—either the performer of the action or the receiver of the action.

SUBJECTS AND PREDICATES

Recall that a sentence has two parts, a **complete subject** and a **complete predicate**, and expresses a complete thought. The subject is the part of the sentence about which something is said.

Examples:

- *My good friend, Harry,* told me a secret.

- *Our city* appears to be clean and beautiful.

- *This table* is made of wood.

- *His Christian faith* gives him moral courage.

The predicate is the part that says something about the subject.

Examples:

■ My good friend, Harry, *told me a secret.*

■ Our city *appears to be clean and beautiful.*

■ This table *is made of wood.*

■ His Christian faith *gives him moral courage.*

 **In each sentence, underline the complete subject once and the complete predicate twice.** *Caution*: The subject does not always come at the beginning of a sentence.

3.1   The lamp is on the table.

3.2   On the table is the lamp.

3.3   I read a good book.

3.4   Bill and Mark played ping pong.

3.5   Coming down the street was Mr. Jones.

The complete subject has a simple subject. The simple subject is the most important word in the complete subject, the word that names the person, place, thing, or idea about which something is said. This word will usually be a noun or a pronoun.

Examples:

■ Her beautiful <u>dress</u> is pink and white.

■ <u>I</u> like to watch birds.

(When the subject is only one word, that word is both the simple subject and the complete subject.)

In these sentences underline the complete subject once and the simple subject twice.

3.6   This old radio works very well.

3.7   I am tired.

3.8   Walking on the roof were two birds.

3.9   There is my new bicycle.

3.10   Jack caught the ball.

The complete predicate has a simple predicate. The simple predicate is the most important word in the complete predicate, a verb or a verb phrase. A verb phrase is a main verb with any helping verbs.

Examples:

■ She <u>will go</u> to the store for me.

■ Mark <u>caught</u> a fish.

■ Today <u>is</u> cold.

■ He <u>has been</u> sick.

✎ **In these sentences underline the complete predicate once and the simple predicate twice.**

3.11   Sue closed the door.

3.12   The chairs are new.

3.13   She will bake cookies.

3.14   We will be coming to your house.

3.15   The children are playing in the yard.

COMPLEMENTS

A sentence can have a third part called a **complement**.

Note: A complement is part of the complete predicate.

The complement is a word or expression used to complete the idea begun by the subject and verb.

Examples:

- The boy likes *peanuts*.

- (The words *The boy* is the complete subject, and the words *likes peanuts* is the complete predicate. The verb *likes* is the simple predicate, and the word *peanuts* is the complement.)

- She is *happy*.

- The children sang a *song*.

✎ **Analyze this sentence.** The old man is eating a simple supper.

3.16   Which words are the complete subject? _____

3.17   Which words are the complete predicate? _____

3.18   Which word is the simple subject? _____

3.19   Which verb phrase is the simple predicate? _____

3.20   Which word is the complement? _____

In each sentence underline the complete predicate once, the simple predicate twice, and the complement three times.

3.21   This month has been long.

3.22   My uncle drives a new car.

3.23   Bob, bring your books.

3.24   Steve can play the trumpet.

3.25   The children watched the animals.

A complement that refers to the simple subject of a sentence is called a subject complement.

Examples:

■ Her name is *Alice*.

■ I am *tall*.

When a noun or pronoun is the subject complement, it is called a **predicate nominative**. A predicate nominative either renames or means the same as the subject.

Examples:

■ She is my *friend*.

■ This is *he*.

As you have already learned, when an adjective is the subject complement, it is called a **predicate adjective**. A predicate adjective modifies the subject.

Examples:

■ The tree is *large*.

■ My bicycle is *blue*.

Two other complements that commonly appear in good sentences with action verbs are objects of the verb. An object can be either an **indirect object** or **direct object**. An indirect object is a noun or a pronoun that tells whom or for whom something is done. A direct object is a noun or a pronoun that receives the action expressed by the verb. A sentence can have a direct object without an indirect object, but it cannot have an indirect object without a direct object. If a sentence has an indirect object, it will come before the direct object.

Examples:

　　　　　　　　　i.o.　　　　d.o.
■ Jim threw <u>Gene</u> the <u>ball</u>.

Gene is the indirect object; the ball was thrown to Gene.
Ball is the direct object; the ball was thrown.

　　　　　　　　　　　d.o.
■ Gene hit the <u>*ball*</u>.

Ball is the direct object; the ball was hit.

 Write true or false.

3.26 _____ A word in the predicate that either renames or modifies the subject is called a subject complement.

3.27 _____ A subject complement refers only to the adjective in a sentence.

3.28 _____ An indirect object receives the action expressed by the verb.

3.29 _____ A direct object tells to whom or for whom something is done.

3.30 _____ The predicate adjective functions as an adjective and is separated from the subject by a verb.

3.31 _____ A noun or a pronoun that is the subject complement is called a predicate nominative.

Write two sentences for each activity.

3.32 Write two sentences that use subject complements. The complement should be a noun that refers to the simple subject. Use an adjective before the complement.

a. _____

b. _____

3.33 Write two sentences that use subject complements. The complement should be a pronoun. Do *not* use an adjective before the complement.

a. _____

b. _____

3.34 Write two sentences that use subject complements. The complements should be adjectives.

a. _____

b. _____

3.35 Write two sentences that use direct objects. The complements should be nouns or pronouns.

a. _____

b. _____

MODIFIERS

Modifiers are words that change, limit, describe, or explain. Adjective modifiers modify nouns or pronouns. Adverb modifiers modify verbs, adjectives, or other adverbs. Modifiers may be words, phrases, or clauses. Prepositional phrases function as either modifiers or adverb modifiers.

Adjectives. A word or phrase that modifies a noun or pronoun is called an adjective.

An adjective will tell *which* one.

Examples:
- That bicycle belongs to Janet.
- The other book is better.
- The second answer is wrong.
- Also: *a*, *an*, and *the* (called articles) a book, an apple, the people

An adjective will tell *how many.*

Examples:
- *Three* boys helped her.
- *Each* person did his own work.
- A *few* dollars will be enough.

An adjective will tell *what kind.*

Examples:
- The *red* flower has a *nice* scent.
- The *big* boy is strong.
- The *tall* lady wears a *long* dress.

In all the examples of adjectives you have seen so far, the adjective comes before the noun or pronoun. Adjectives can come after a noun, although this position is unusual.

An adjective can come immediately after a noun.

Examples:

- The puppy, *cute* and *fluffy*, played with his tail.
- The child, *sleepy* and *tired*, was soon asleep.

An adjective can be part of the predicate (called a predicate adjective).

Examples:

- Today is *beautiful*.
- The flower is *red*.
- The food is *plentiful*.

What kind? Which one? How many?

Underline the complete subject once and the adjectives twice.
Draw a third line under predicate adjectives.

3.36   Five cookies are on the table.

3.37   The small boy is afraid of dogs.

3.38   Kathy is helpful.

3.39   A second look will be helpful.

3.40   The boys, rude and loud, demanded milk.

3.41   Keith and Werner are big and strong.

3.42   The old man is tired.

3.43   An apple tastes good.

3.44   A few girls, only three, have ice skates.

3.45   That man is funny.

Write three sentences for each activity.

3.46   Write three sentences with an adjective before each simple subject.
The adjective should tell *how many*.

a. _____

b. _____

c. _____

3.47   Write three sentences with an adjective before each simple subject.
The adjective should tell *which one*.

a. _____

b. _____

c. _____

3.48   Write three sentences with an adjective before each simple subject.
The adjective should tell *what kind*.

a. _____

b. _____

c. _____

Write a paragraph using as many descriptive words (adjectives) that seem appropriate.

3.49 Choose a topic sentence:

1. A good breakfast is easy to cook.

2. Money cannot buy the best things in life.

TEACHER CHECK _____ _____
                                    initials   date

Adverbs. A word that modifies the simple predicate (verb) is called an adverb. An adverb will tell *when*.

Examples:

- John, do your homework *now*.
- I *always* say grace.
- We go to church *weekly*.

An adverb will tell *where*.

Examples:

- She lives *there*.
- Sue will lie *down* and take a nap.
- *Here* are the cookies.

An adverb will tell how.

Examples:

- Joe *quickly* ran across the field.
- Are you feeling *poorly*?
- She skated as *fast* as she could.

An adverb will tell *how much.*

Examples:

- I will *not* write a poem.
- Will it take *long*?
- I *almost* went to Hawaii.

An adverb can modify *another* adverb.

Examples:

- She runs *very* quickly.
- She has *never* before attempted to play the violin.
- Jill can jump *quite* high.

An adverb can modify an adjective.

Examples:

- The room is *not* clean.
- She is a *very* good singer.
- Today is *too* hot.

Underline the adverbs once and the words they modify twice. If the word being modified also modifies another word, underline it three times. Identify the word being modified by writing above it: *V* for verb, *Adv* for adverb, and *Adj* for adjective.

Adj.
Example: My teacher is very smart.

3.50 I never use profanity.

3.51 Mark sits there.

3.52 Phil carefully drew a picture of a horse.

3.53 Scott nearly fell from a tree.

3.54 Scott very nearly fell from a tree.

3.55 It's not nice to spit on the sidewalk.

3.56 She quite suddenly became very sad.

Write three sentences for each activity.

3.57 Write three sentences with an adverb before or after each simple predicate. The adverb should tell *when*.

a. _____

b. _____

c. _____

3.58 Write three sentences with an adverb before or after each simple predicate. The adverb should tell *where.*

a. _____

b. _____

c. _____

3.59 Write three sentences with an adverb before or after each simple predicate. The adverb should tell *how.*

a. _____

b. _____

c. _____

3.60   Write three sentences in which an adverb modifies another adverb.

a. _____

b. _____

c. _____

3.61   Write three sentences in which an adverb modifies an adjective.
The adverb should tell *how much*.

a. _____

b. _____

c. _____

3.62   Write a sentence that uses the adverb *not*.

_____

_____

Write true or false.

3.63   _____   Adjectives tell which one, what kind, and how many.

3.64   _____   Adjectives always precede (come before) the subject of a sentence.

3.65   _____   Sometimes an adjective is part of the predicate.

3.66   _____   Adverbs may modify verbs only.

We have studied that a sentence must have two parts: a subject and a predicate. These two parts form the **core** of a sentence. The core of a sentence can also have a third part, a complement. The subject and predicate parts are always required. The complement is not always required.

Prepositional phrases. A **preposition** is a word that joins a noun or pronoun to some other word in a sentence.

Examples:

- She goes *to* the library.

- She goes *by* the library

- She goes *in* the library.

The preposition *to, by*, and *in* join the noun *library* with the verb *goes.*

Study the following list of prepositions so that you will be very familiar with them.

Common Prepositions			
above	between	into	to
across	by	like	toward
after	down	of	under
at	during	off	until
before	except	on	up
behind	for	out	upon
below	from	over	with
beside	in	through	without

A prepositional phrase is a group of words that begins with a preposition and ends with a noun or pronoun.

Examples:

■ I will go *to the store*.

■ Jill went *across the street*.

■ She played the piano *during lunch*.

■ Go *without me*.

■ *One of the boys* is sick.

 Underline the prepositional phrase once and the preposition twice.

3.67 Myron ran down the stairs.

3.68 He came over the hill and through the garden.

3.69 She will come to our house in the morning.

3.70 On the table is the book.

3.71 One of the girls brought some candy for you.

A prepositional phrase can do the work of an adjective.

Examples:

■ The *hall* closet is full. (adjective)

■ The closet *in the hall* is full. (prep. phrase)

■ Here is the *dog* food. (adjective)

■ Here is the food *for the dog*. (prep. phrase)

Rewrite each sentence. Substitute a prepositional phrase for the underlined adjectives.

3.72   The <u>bedroom</u> floor is dirty. _____

_____

3.73   The <u>Phoenix</u> basketball team plays well. _____

_____

3.74   We need <u>baseball</u> gloves. _____

_____

3.75   They have <u>circus</u> tickets. _____

_____

3.76   John watched a <u>basketball</u> game. _____

_____

A prepositional phrase can do the work of an adverb.

Examples:

■ I swam *in the* water. (Tells where I swam)

■ I swam *after lunch*. (Tells when I swam)

■ I swam *on my back.* (Tells how I swam)

■ I swam *for a short time.* (Tells how much I swam)

Write two sentences for each activity.

3.77   Write two sentences with adverb prepositional phrases that tell when something was done.

a. _____

b. _____

3.78   Write two sentences with adverb prepositional phrases that tell where something was done.

a. _____

b. _____

3.79   Write two sentences with adverb prepositional phrases that tell how something was done.

a. _____

b. _____

3.80 Write two sentences with adverb prepositional phrases that tell how much something was done.

a. _____

b. _____

Complete this activity.

3.81 Choose one of these topic sentences and write a paragraph using adjectives, adverbs, and prepositional phrases.

1. I believe in miracles.

2. Sometimes I don't like myself.

TEACHER CHECK _____ _____

initials   date

![circular arrow icon] **Review the material in this section in preparation for the Self Test.** This Self Test will check your mastery of this particular section as well as your knowledge of all previous sections. The items missed on this Self Test will indicate specific areas where restudy is needed for mastery.

SELF TEST 3

Match these items (each answer, 2 points).

3.01	_____ first word of a sentence	a. capitalized
3.02	_____ first word of a direct quotation	b. not capitalized
3.03	_____ first word of a line of poetry	
3.04	_____ all words in titles	
3.05	_____ all pronouns	

Match these items (each answer, 2 points).

3.06	_____ used with letter *s* to form the possessive case of singular nouns	a. quotation marks
		b. commas
		c. parentheses
3.07	_____ used to join compound numbers and words	d. apostrophe
		e. semicolon
3.08	_____ used to set off nonrestrictive clauses and phrases	f. hyphen
3.09	_____ used with titles of songs and short stories	
3.010	_____ used to show what letters were dropped in a contraction	

Add the correct punctuation marks where needed (each numbered item, 4 points).

3.011 Yes we all sang The Star Spangled Banner.

3.012 You can go with us or you can stay with your cousin.

3.013 Before Joy answered the telephone she closed the door.

3.014 Tonights dinner will include soup salad main course and dessert.

3.015 Father said Jon please come here.

Answer true or false (each answer, 2 points).

3.016 _____ Proper nouns, proper pronouns, and proper adjectives are capitalized.

3.017 _____ Adverbs modify nouns and pronouns.

3.018 _____ Adjectives modify verbs, adverbs, and other adjectives.

3.019 _____ A prepositional phrase begins with a preposition and ends with a noun or a pronoun.

3.020 _____ The subject is the part of the sentence about which something is said.

3.021 _____ An adverb tells which one, how many, or what kind.

3.022 _____ An adjective tells when, where, how, or how much.

3.023 _____ A prepositional phrase functions as an adjective or an adverb.

3.024 _____ A modifier changes, describes, or explains.

3.025 _____ An adverb can modify an adjective.

Write the letter for the correct answer on each line (each answer, 2 points).

3.026 In a sentence the words, *down the stairs*, would be a _____ .
   a. prepositional phrase   b. restrictive phrase
   c. verb phrase

3.027 A word that modifies a simple predicate is called a/an _____ .
   a. adjective   b. adverb   c. phrase

3.028 When an adjective is part of the predicate and modifies the subject, it is called a _____ .
   a. predicate nominative   b. predicate adjective
   c. subjective object

3.029 A word that modifies a simple subject is called a/an _____ .
   a. adverb   b. phrase   c. adjective

3.030 A word in the predicate that either renames or modifies the subject is called a subject

   _____ .
   a. object   b. complement   c. modifier

Complete these statements (each answer, 3 points).

3.031 The part of a sentence about which something is told is called the _____ .

3.032 The part of a sentence that receives the action expressed by the verb is called a direct

_____ .

3.033 A group of words that begins with a preposition and ends with a noun or a pronoun

is called a _____ phrase.

3.034 A predicate adjective is a word in the predicate that modifies the _____ .

3.035 A noun or a pronoun that is the subject complement is called a predicate _____ .

Write these sentences (each sentence, 5 points).

3.036 Write a sentence that has a simple subject with at least one modifier in the complete
subject.

_____

3.037 Write a sentence containing a predicate adjective.

_____

3.038 Write a sentence containing a direct object.

_____

4. THE STRUCTURE OF ENGLISH: PART II

A simple sentence is a group of words that contains a subject and a predicate and expresses a complete thought. A clause is a group of words that contains a subject and a predicate and that forms a part of a sentence. An independent, or main clause expresses a complete thought. Notice that a simple sentence and an independent clause have the same description with one exception: An independent clause forms a part of a sentence. Clauses form compound sentences, complex sentences, and compound-complex sentences. Two important words to these kinds of sentences are *coordination* and *subordination*. In this section of Language Arts LIFEPAC 706, you will study the meanings and uses of these two terms.

SECTION OBJECTIVES

Review these objectives. When you have completed this section, you should be able to:

7. Describe and correctly use coordination when writing.
8. Identify and correctly use subordination when writing.
9. Identify and correctly use relative clauses when writing.
11. Spell new words.
12. Write clear sentences.

VOCABULARY

Study these words to enhance your learning success in this section.

conjunctive adverb (kun jungk' tiv ad' verb). Adverbs that join groups of words; examples include *nevertheless, however,* and *moreover*.

coordinating conjunction (ko ôr' du nāt ing kun jungk' shun). A word that joins words, phrases, or clauses of equal value; examples include *and, but,* and *for*.

equal (ē' kwul). The same in amount or value.

related (ri lā' tid). Connected.

relationship (ri lā' shun ship). Connection.

subordinating conjunction (su bôr' du nāt ing kun jungk' shun). A word that joins a less important idea to a more important idea; examples include *because, if,* and *whether*.

COORDINATION

The term "language elements" will be used in this section. A language element can be a noun, a pronoun, a verb, an adjective, or an adverb. It can also be a phrase or a clause. Coordination is the compounding, or joining, of two or more **equal** language elements. Good writers use coordination.

When something is compound, it has two or more parts. When a writer uses coordination, he uses two or more language elements that are closely **related**. A compound element usually has a minimum of three words: two equal language elements and a conjunction, such as *and* or *or*.

Compound nouns and pronouns. Nouns and pronouns can be compounded. Nouns, proper nouns, and personal pronouns can be mixed, if their **relationship** is equal. That is, nouns, proper nouns, and personal pronouns can be mixed only if they are used as the same part of the sentence—subject or object, for example.

Nouns

Examples:

■ men and women

■ mountain and lake

■ chair or stool

Proper nouns

Examples:

■ Bill and Sally

■ Texas or Alaska

Personal pronouns

Examples:

■ he and she

■ you or me

■ we and they

Nouns, proper nouns, and pronouns mixed

Examples:

■ She and Doreen are cute.

■ I will give it to the boy or him.

■ Bill and his father went on a camping trip.

Compound verbs, adjectives, and adverbs. Verbs, adjectives, and adverbs can also be compounded. These sentence elements can only be compounded with a sentence element of the same kind—verb with verb, adjective with adjective, adverb with adverb.

Verbs

Examples:

■ *run* and *jump*

■ *sat* or *stood*

■ *walked* or *jogged*

Adjectives

Examples:

■ *happy* and *glad*

■ *one* or *two* (people)

■ *red* and *green*

Adverbs

Examples:

■ *slowly* and *carefully*

■ *now* or *later*

■ *here* and *there*

Coordinate (compound) each language element. Do not mix nouns, proper nouns, or personal pronouns with verbs, adjectives, and adverbs.

4.1 ham and _____

4.2 he and _____

4.3 France or _____

4.4 laugh or _____

4.5 talked and _____

4.6 was and _____

4.7 sad and _____

4.8 second or _____

4.9 quietly or _____

4.10 (jump) up and _____

You studied that the core of a sentence consists of a subject, a predicate, and sometimes a complement. When the core of a sentence has a complement, it is part of the complete predicate. Examples: (1) Mary felt happy. *Mary* is the subject and *felt happy* is the complete predicate. *Happy* is the complement. (2) Bob hit the ball. *Bob* is the subject, *hit the ball* is the complete predicate, and *ball* is the complement.

Compound subjects, predicates, and complements. Language elements can be used in coordination.

The subject can be compounded.

Examples:

■ *Matthew, Mark, Luke, and John* are the four Gospel writers.

■ *Tennis* and *soccer* are forms of recreation.

■ *Sugar or honey* can be used.

What is wrong with this sentence? Tennis and hiking are *forms of recreation*. The compound subjects *tennis and hiking* do not have an equal relationship or meaning. Tennis is a form of competitive recreation, but hiking may be done individually. Do not coordinate subjects unless they are closely related, as in the sentence: *Tennis and soccer are forms of recreation.*

The simple predicate (verb) can be compounded.

Examples:

■ I can *run and jump*.

■ She *knits and sews* quite well.

■ He *drives or walks* to school.

The complete predicate can be compounded.

Examples:

■ He *drives to school* and *walks home*. (ways to travel)

■ She *vacuumed the carpet* and *washed the windows.* (housework)

■ Brent *kicked the ball, ran fifty yards, and tackled the runner.* (actions in a football game)

Caution! Do not compound predicates that are not closely related. You would not want to write, "She rode her bicycle and picked flowers," unless both occurred at the same time.

A complement can be compounded.

Examples:

■ We ate *cake and ice cream.*

■ The sofa is *blue and green.*

■ Do you know *him or her*?

More than one part of a sentence core can be compounded.

Examples:

■ *Dick and Ricardo threw and caught* the baseball. (Compound subject and predicate)

■ *Dick and Ricardo will go to town or stay at home*. (Compound subject and complete predicate)

■ *Dick and Ricardo* ate *popcorn and peanuts*. (Compound subject and complement)

Write two sentences for each activity.

4.11   Compound the subject.

a. _____

b. _____

4.12   Compound the simple predicate.

a. _____

b. _____

4.13   Compound the complete predicate.

a. _____

b. _____

4.14   Compound the complement.

a. _____

b. _____

4.15   Compound both the simple subject and the simple predicate.

a. _____

b. _____

4.16   Compound both the simple subject and the complete predicate.

a. _____

b. _____

4.17   Compound both the subject and the complement.

a. _____

b. _____

Compound modifiers. Language elements that modify can be used in coordination.

Adjectives that modify the subject can be compounded.

Examples:

- The *cute and fluffy* puppy wagged his tail.
- Also: The *cute, fluffy, and friendly* puppy wagged his tail.

- The baby, *wet and hungry*, cried for his mother.

Adjectives that modify the complement can be compounded.

Examples:

- Mother gave me a *red and juicy* apple.
- My brother will tell a *funny or* a *scary* story.

Adverbs that modify the simple predicate can be compounded.

Examples:

- Jim practiced *long* and *hard*.

- She *carefully and patiently* painted the shells.

- Will you go *now or later*?

 Complete these activities.

4.18 Write a sentence with two or more adjectives that modify the subject.

_____

4.19 Write a sentence with two or more adjectives that modify the complement.

_____

4.20 Write a sentence with two or more adverbs before the simple predicate.

_____

Complete this activity.

4.21 Write a paragraph using as many compound combinations as possible. Review the compounds studied up to now. Choose a topic sentence:

1. My little brother is always pretending.

2. I never tire of going to the zoo.

 **TEACHER CHECK** _____ _____

initials   date

Compound phrases. A phrase is a group of words that work together to form a single part of speech. A phrase can have a subject or a verb, but it cannot have both. If you want to compound an adjective phrase, you must use another adjective phrase. You cannot mix an adjective phrase with a noun phrase, a verb phrase, or an adverb phrase when you use coordination.

Prepositional phrases can be compounded.

Examples:

- I will arrive *in the morning* or *in the afternoon*. (adverb phrases)

- Dick jumped *into the air* and *over the fence*. (adverb phrases)

A subject with a prepositional phrase can be compounded.

Example: T*he man from Denver* and the *lady from Kansas City* lost their luggage. (compound subjects with prepositional phrases that act as adjectives)

A simple predicate with a prepositional phrase can be compounded.

Example: Nicky *sat in a chair* and *looked at a magazine*.

A participial phrase can be compounded.

Example: *Standing on a ladder* and *looking over the fence*, Hans could see his friends.

Infinitive phrases can be compounded.

Example: I like to *read books*, to *talk with friends*, and *to be relaxed*.

Compound the underlined phrase in each sentence. In the space provided, write a similar kind of phrase.

Example: Eating in restaurants and staying at motels, Father wished his business trip was over.

4.22 I will be at school or _____

4.23 The pen with the blue ink and _____

4.24 Jamie lay in her bed and _____

4.25 Sitting on a bench and _____

Steve waited for his friends.

4.26 Mark likes to eat, to sleep, and _____

Complete this activity.

4.27 Write six sentences with compound phrases.

a. _____

b. _____

c. _____

d. _____

e. _____

f. _____

Compound subordinate clauses. Subordinate clauses can be used in coordination.

Recall that a clause is a group of words that has a subject and a predicate. A clause is used as part of a sentence. A subordinate (or dependent) clause does not express a complete idea. It depends on an independent (main) clause; that is, it must be linked, or joined, to an independent clause in a sentence. It is joined to an independent clause by a subordinating conjunction (when, if, where, for example).

Look at this clause: When I am older... This clause has a subject (I) and a verb (am), but it is not a complete idea. It needs to be joined to an independent clause.

Look at this clause: I would like to be a doctor... This clause has a subject and a verb. It expresses a complete idea, and it could be a sentence. It is an independent clause. It does not depend on another clause. If you wish, you can add subordinate clauses to this independent clause. The subordinate clause, when

I am older, can be added to the end of the independent clause I would like to be a doctor with this result:

- I would like to be a doctor when I am older.

The subordinate clause can be placed before the independent clause, but a comma must now be used to separate the two clauses:

- When I am older, I would like to be a doctor.

The last sentence is a good example of subordination, which you will study later. Like other language elements, subordinate clauses can be compound if two or more clauses have an equal relationship. A subordinate clause can show many relationships. The most important relationships are these:

- time
- place
- cause
- requirement

Subordinate clauses that show a time relationship begin with these words (subordinating conjunctions): before, after, when, until, while.

Examples:

- when I was young
- after the game was over
- while you are away

Subordinate clauses that show a place relationship begin with these words (subordinating conjunctions): where, wherever.

Examples:

- where the lilies grow
- wherever you are

Subordinate clauses that show a cause relationship begin with these words (subordinating conjunctions): because, since, as.

Examples:

- because it is cold
- since you wish to go
- as I am sick

Subordinate clauses that show a requirement relationship begin with these words (subordinating conjunctions): if, unless.

Examples:

- if it is possible
- unless you try

When compounding subordinate clauses, do not mix relationships.

- Wrong: When I am older and if I am smart enough, I would like to be a doctor. (combines time and requirement relationships)
- Correct: When I am older and after I am ready, I would like to be a doctor. (combines time relationships)

Note: The first sentence is not wrong as far as grammar is concerned. It is only wrong as far as coordination is concerned.

Compound the underlined subordinate clauses in each sentence. In the space provided, write a subordinate clause that has a similar relationship (time, place, cause or requirement).

4.28   I am wearing a jacket <u>since the weather</u> is cold and _____

_____ .

4.29   I will go with you <u>if I finish my homework</u> and _____

_____ .

Complete this activity.

4.30 Write sentences that use two or more subordinate clauses and show each kind of relation-ship: time, place, cause, and requirement. You will write four sentences.

a. _____

b. _____

c. _____

d. _____

Compound sentences. When two or more independent clauses are joined, a compound sentence is formed.

You have studied that an independent (main) clause has a subject and a predicate. It expresses a complete idea, and it can stand alone as a sentence. It is possible to join two independent clauses in one sentence. Such a sentence is called a *compound sentence.* Before you study about coordinating independent clauses, you will need to know how two inde-pendent clauses are joined. When two indepen-dent clauses are joined, the following kinds of tools are used:

1. comma
2. semicolon
3. coordinating conjunction
4. conjunctive adverb

You know what a comma is, of course. A semi-colon looks like this;

These words are coordinating conjunctions: *and, or, nor, but, for, yet,* and *so.*

The most common conjunctive adverbs are *furthermore, in addition, indeed, in fact, likewise, moreover, instead, nevertheless, therefore, conse-quently, thus, however,* and *hence.*

Two independent clauses can be joined by using a coordinating conjunction. A *comma* is placed before the coordinating conjunction.

Examples:

■ The sun was shining brightly, and the sun was hot.

■ I will go to the mountains, or I will drive to the desert.

Note: If the two independent clauses are very short, a comma is not used.

Example: She worked and he played.

When a comma and the coordinating conjunc-tion and are used to join two independent clauses, a semicolon can be used in their place.

Example: The sun was shining brightly; the day was hot. (Remember! Do not use a semicolon if a coordinating conjunction other than *and* is to be substituted.)

Two independent clauses can be joined by a conjunctive adverb. A semicolon is placed before the conjunctive adverb. A comma usu-ally is placed after it.

Examples:

■ Today is very cold; *in fact,* it is the coldest day in twenty years. (A comma is needed.)

■ Today is very cold; therefore, you should dress warmly.

Section 4 | 63

 Complete these activities.

4.31 Join the following independent clauses. Use a comma and a coordinating conjunction.

a. The old man sat quietly, _____ he watched the children play.

b. I will bake cookies, _____ I might make a fruit salad.

c. Using this technique, write a sentence of your own.

_____

_____

4.32 Join the following independent clauses with a semicolon.

a. The birds fly south for the winter they return in the spring.

b. I like dogs I also like cats.

c. Using this technique, write a sentence of your own.

_____

_____

4.33 Join the following independent clauses. Use a semicolon and a conjunctive adverb. Use a comma after the conjunctive adverb.

a. Sue spent all of her money _____ she cannot afford to go ice skating.

b. The price of food is high _____ it is higher than it has ever been.

c. Using this technique, write a sentence of your own.

_____

_____

Language elements such as independent clauses can also be used in coordination.

When you write a *compound* sentence, the independent clauses must have a relationship. If the clauses are not related to each other, they should not be joined in the same sentence. Using two separate sentences would be better. Compare these two compound sentences:

- *Brenda is pretty*, but *she is not conceited.*

- *Brenda is pretty*, and *she likes to eat popcorn.*

The first sentence is logical because the two clauses work together. The two clauses in the second sentence are not related. Brenda's appearance has nothing to do with her fondness for popcorn. The following changes would make the clauses work together: *Brenda likes to eat popcorn and other fattening foods,* yet *she remains in slender form.*

SUBORDINATION

We know that a language element can be a word, a phrase, a subordinate clause, or an independent clause. When equal language elements are joined, we have coordination. When we join language elements that are not equal, we have subordination. One very important thing about subordination is also important to coordination. In subordination the language elements are not equal, but they have a relationship. In subordination you will have one important idea and one or more ideas that are less important. The less important idea will add emphasis to the important idea. The less important idea may also modify the important idea.

What is the purpose of subordination and coordination? Why should we use them in our writing? Read this paragraph:

- My uncle is generous and kind. He bought me a new tennis racket. He then took me to a restaurant. We had a delicious meal. I have many relatives. My uncle is my favorite.

Now read this paragraph:

- Generous and kind, my uncle bought me a new tennis racket, and then he took me to a restaurant where we had a delicious meal. Of all my many relatives, my uncle is my favorite.

Both paragraphs express the same ideas. The first paragraph has only simple sentences (one independent clause for each) and sounds somewhat choppy. The second paragraph has coordination and subordination. It sounds mature, has good variety, and is more interesting to read.

Read this paragraph:

- My uncle is generous and kind, and he bought me a new tennis racket. He took me to a restaurant, and we had a delicious meal. I have many relatives, but my uncle is my favorite.

Although this paragraph is better than the first, it sounds like a teeter-totter. All the sentences have two independent clauses. The paragraph has very little variety, and it uses too much coordination.

A good writer uses a combination of simple sentences, subordination, and coordination. You know how to write simple sentences. You also know how to use words, phrases, and clauses in coordination. If you can learn how to use subordination, you will be a better writer.

Subordinate clauses. Subordinate clauses can be added to an independent clause.

Use a comma if the subordinate clause comes at the beginning of a sentence.

Examples:

- *When we finished breakfast*, our family went to a lake.

- *Though they are difficult*, I like to read the classics.

Do not use a comma if the subordinate clause is at the end of a sentence unless it is not essential to the meaning of the sentence.

Examples:

- Our family went to the lake *when we finished breakfast*. (essential to the meaning)

- I like to read the classics, *although they are difficult*. (not essential)

Some subordinate clauses modify the main verb in an independent clause (adverb clause).

Examples:

- *Because he was late for the game*, Johnny (came thundering) into the house.

- Mother (did not eat) *until everyone had been served.*

Some subordinate clauses modify the subject of an independent clause (adjective clause).

Examples:

- Bill, *who won the spelling contest*, jumped up and down.

- Jane, *who was standing on her head*, pretended she was walking on the ceiling.

- The dog *that is sitting on the floor* is mine.

Some subordinate clauses act as nouns and give special meaning or emphasis to the subject or complement of an independent clause (noun clause). *Note:* Noun clauses do not usually require commas. They usually begin with these words: *who, what, why, which, that, how, where, whether, whatever, or whoever.*

Examples:

- *Why Christ died* is explained in the Bible. (used as the subject)

- We learned *how birds build nests*. (used as a complement)

 Complete these sentences.

4.34 Add a subordinate clause that modifies the main verb of the independent clause:

I *will* not go _____ .

4.35 Add a subordinate clause that modifies the main verb of the independent clause:

_____ , Bob *ran* to the store.

4.36 Add a subordinate clause that modifies the subject of the independent clause:

Mrs. Smith, _____ , rested for awhile.

4.37 Add a subordinate clause that modifies the subject of the independent clause:

The *man* _____ , is my father.

4.38 Add a noun clause: _____ , was the topic of the program.

Complex sentence. A complex sentence has one independent clause (*IND CL*) and one or more subordinate clauses (SUB CL).

Examples:

- SUB CL + *IND CL*: When you return, *I will be here.*

- *IND* CL + SUB CL: *I will be here* when you return.

- SUB CL + *IND CL* + SUB CL: When you return, *I will be here* if it's not too late.

- SUB CL + SUB CL + *IND CL*: If it's not too late when you return, *I will be here.*

- *IND CL* + SUB CL + SUB CL: *I will be here* when you return if it's not too late.

Write two complex sentences for each pattern.

4.39 SUB CL + *IND CL*: a. _____

_____

b. _____

4.40 *IND CL* + SUB CL: a. _____

_____

b. _____

4.41 SUB CL + *IND CL* + SUB CL: a. _____

_____

b. _____

4.42 SUB CL + SUB CL + *IND CL*: a. _____

_____

b. _____

4.43 *IND CL* + SUB CL + SUB CL: a. _____

_____

b. _____

Note: *When the subordinate clauses have the same relationship to the independent clause, it's coordination. Otherwise, it's subordination.*

Compound-complex sentence. A compound-complex sentence has two independent clauses and one or more subordinate clauses.

Examples:

- SUB CL + *IND CL* + *IND CL*: When you return, *I will be here,* and *I will make you a sandwich.*

- *IND CL* + *IND CL* + SUB CL: *I will be here,* and *I will make you a sandwich when you return.*

- *IND CL* + SUB CL + *IND CL*: *I will be here* when you return, and *I will make you a sandwich.*

Write two compound-complex sentences for each pattern.

4.44 SUB CL + IND CL + IND:

    a. _____

    b. _____

4.45 IND CL + IND CL + SUB CL:

    a. _____

    b. _____

4.46 IND CL + SUB CL + IND CL:

    a. _____

    b. _____

Complete this activity.

4.47 Write a paragraph after choosing one of the following topic sentences:

1. Personally, I like watching football games.

2. Jogging is an excellent way to stay in shape.

3. Saturdays are very special days to me.

As you write your paragraph, use at least two compound sentences and two compound-complex sentences.

TEACHER CHECK _____ _____

                                    initials   date

Relative clauses. A relative clause is a subordinate clause. It has a verb and its subject, but it does not express a complete idea. A relative clause does the work of an adjective.

A relative clause begins with a relative pronoun. The most common relative pronouns are *who, whom, whose, that,* and *which*. A relative pronoun relates, or refers, to another word in a sentence. That other word is called an antecedent. It is called an antecedent because it is a word that usually comes before the relative pronoun. The antecedent is a noun or a pronoun, and it is usually the subject or object in a sentence. The antecedent is modified by the relative clause.

Review these functions of a relative clause.

1. A relative clause is a subordinate clause.

2. A relative clause does the work of an adjective.

3. A relative clause begins with a relative pronoun such as *who, whom, whose, that,* or *which*.

4. A relative clause refers to and modifies an antecedent.

5. An antecedent is the subject or object complement in a sentence that comes before the relative clause.

The relative pronouns *who, whom,* and *whose* refer to people.

Examples:

- The man who came to dinner is my uncle.

- Edna is the girl whom you want.

- The girl whose dog is lost is offering a reward.

The relative pronoun *which* refers to *things.*

- **Example**: A car which has a canvas top is called a convertible.

The relative pronoun *that* refers to *people* or *things.*

Examples:

- The baseball team *that won the pennant last year* is now in second place. (people)

- Apples that are green are usually sour. (things)

Use the relative pronoun *who* if it is used as the subject of a verb.

Examples:

- The boy who borrowed my coat is my friend.

- The girls who went to camp will return on Friday. (The subject can be singular or plural.)

Use the relative pronoun *whom* if it is used as the object of a verb.

Example: This is the boy whom you saw. (*You* is the subject, *saw* is the verb, and *whom* is the object)

Jan and Murry ate their lunch.

Underline the relative clause in each sentence once and the antecedent twice.

4.48   Dogs that bark annoy me.

4.49   I like candy that is sour.

4.50   People whose minds are on the Lord usually lead good lives.

4.51   John is a person whom we like.

       Note: The antecedent comes immediately before the relative clause.

Write two sentences for each activity.

4.52   Use a relative clause that begins with the relative pronoun *that* and modifies either the subject or the object.

      a. _____

      b. _____

4.53   Use a relative clause that begins with *who* and modifies the subject.

      a. _____

      b. _____

4.54   Use a relative clause that begins with *which* and modifies the subject or the object.

      a. _____

      b. _____

4.55   Use a relative clause that begins with *whose* and modifies either the subject or the object.

      a. _____

      b. _____

4.56   Use a relative clause that begins with *whom* and modifies the object.

      a. _____

      b. _____

Complete this activity.

4.57 Choose a topic sentence and write a paragraph:

1. My favorite clothes are fall and winter clothes.

2. Hiking is my favorite pastime.

In this paragraph, use relative clauses.

TEACHER CHECK _____ _____
initials   date

SPELLING

Correct spelling of words is only one skill for writing clear and meaningful sentences. A good understanding of the meaning of the words helps you to write intelligently. A knowledge of synonyms also makes writing more interesting to read.

Spelling Words-3		
abundance	definitely	license
acquaintance	desperate	loneliness
amateur	efficient	marriage
bargain	foreign	municipal
beautiful	gasoline	orchestra
business	government	pleasant
calendar	handkerchief	restaurant
column	initial	rhythm
conquer		

Complete these activities.

4.58 List fifteen of the words from Spelling Words-3.
In the opposite column write one synonym for each word.

Word	Synonym
a. _____	_____
b. _____	_____
c. _____	_____
d. _____	_____
e. _____	_____
f. _____	_____
g. _____	_____
h. _____	_____
i. _____	_____
j. _____	_____
k. _____	_____
l. _____	_____
m. _____	_____
n. _____	_____
o. _____	_____

4.59 Write fifteen sentences using each of these words. Include the synonyms if you can.
Also, incorporate some of the knowledge you gained from this LIFEPAC.

_____

_____

_____

_____

_____

_____

_____

_____

_____

_____

_____

_____

_____

_____

_____

_____

_____

_____

_____

_____

_____

_____

TEACHER CHECK _____ _____
                                           initials   date

ABC **Ask your teacher to give you a practice spelling test of Spelling Words-3.** Restudy the words you missed.

Before you take this last Self Test, you may want to do one or more of these self checks.

1. _____ Read the objectives. See if you can do them.
2. _____ Restudy the material related to any objectives that you cannot do.
3. _____ Use the **SQ3R** study procedure to review the material:
   a. **S**can the sections.
   b. **Q**uestion yourself.
   c. **R**ead to answer your questions.
   d. **R**ecite the answers to yourself.
   e. **R**eview areas you did not understand.
4. _____ Review all vocabulary, activities, and Self Tests, writing a correct answer for every wrong answer.

SELF TEST 4

Answer true or false (each answer, 1 point).

4.01 _____ Both commas and parentheses are used to set off parenthetic expressions.

4.02 _____ Proper pronouns, proper nouns, and proper adjectives are not capitalized.

4.03 _____ Adverbs modify verbs, adjectives, and other adverbs.

4.04 _____ Adjectives modify nouns and pronouns.

4.05 _____ A prepositional phrase begins with a preposition and ends with a verb.

For each item write *N* for noun, *V* for verb, *Adj* for adjective, *Adv* for adverb, and *P* for preposition (each answer, 3 points).

4.06 _____ modifies the simple predicate

4.07 _____ used to modify the simple subject

4.08 _____ what the simple subject is

4.09 _____ what the simple predicate is

4.010 _____ examples are *to, in, around,* and *by*

4.011 _____ tells which one, how many, or what kind

4.012 _____ tells when, where, how, or how much

4.013 _____ a word that joins a noun or pronoun to some other word in a sentence

4.014 _____ the antecedent of a relative clause.

4.015 _____ other than a subject, what a clause must have

Match these items (each answer, 2 points).

4.016 _____ comma

4.017 _____ semicolon

4.018 _____ subordinating conjunctions

4.019 _____ coordinating conjunctions

4.020 _____ subordination

4.021 _____ coordination

4.022 _____ relative pronouns

4.023 _____ conjunctive adverbs

a. nevertheless, therefore

b. who, that, which

c. his, her, their

d. often used with coordinating conjunctions

e. the joining of language elements that are not equal

f. because, if

g. often used with conjunctive adverbs

h. the joining of equal language elements

i. and, but

Decide if each sentence is an example of subordination or coordination. Write *C* for coordination and *S* for subordination (each answer, 3 points).

4.024 _____ Jack will go to the ocean, and Heather will go to the mountains.

4.025 _____ When she was a young girl, my mother lived on a farm.

4.026 _____ Because I play the trumpet well, I am going to join a band since it is something I will enjoy.

4.027 _____ Janet's mother wants her to be a nurse, but her father wants her to be a teacher.

Capitalize and punctuate each sentence correctly. Add punctuation marks where needed and underline any letter that should be capitalized (each sentence, 3 points).

4.028 jack said, mother, may i have seventy-five cents?

4.029 last wednesday, john and i saw the today show.

4.030 the childrens siamese cat its brown is an all star pest.

4.031 the ladies meeting will be held at the first christian church on august 3.

4.032 steve told us he is studying spanish at cleveland christian school which is located on third street.

4.033 if you want to be successful said father do your best but you should never worry that your best isnt good enough.

Write sentences using these words (each answer, 4 points).

4.034 amateur _____

4.035 efficient _____

4.036 initial _____

4.037 modify _____

4.038 related _____

81 / 101   SCORE _____   TEACHER _____ _____
                                          initials   date

Before taking the LIFEPAC Test, you may want to do one or more of these self checks.

1. _____ Read the objectives. See if you can do them.
2. _____ Restudy the material related to any objectives that you cannot do.
3. _____ Use the **SQ3R** study procedure to review the material.
4. _____ Review activities, Self Tests, and LIFEPAC vocabulary words.
5. _____ Restudy areas of weakness indicated by the last Self Test.